W9-BDI-600

A Spirited Sip of Chicken Soup for the Soul®

In Celebration of Women

Andrews McMeel Publishing

Kansas City

ISBN: 0-8362-5090-7

A Spirited Sip of Chicken Soup for the Soul®

In Celebration of Women

Inspired by the #1 New York Times bestseller

Chicken Soup for the Soul®

by Jack Canfield and Mark Victor Hansen

Miss Hardy

by H. Stephen Glenn

I began life as a learning-disabled child. I had a distortion of vision called dyslexia. Dyslexic children often learn words quickly, but don't know they don't see them the way other people do. I perceived my world as a wonderful place filled with these shapes called words and developed a rather extensive sight vocabulary that made my parents quite optimistic about my ability to learn. To my horror, I discovered in the first grade that letters were more important than words. Dyslexic children make them upside down and backwards, and don't even arrange them in the same order as everybody else. So my first-grade teacher called me learning-disabled.

She wrote down her observations and passed them on to my second-grade teacher over the summer so she could develop an appropriate bias against me before I arrived. I entered the second grade able to see the answers to math problems but having no idea what the busy work was to reach them, and discovered that the busy work was more important than the answer. Now I was totally intimidated by the learning process, so I developed a stutter. Being unable to speak up assertively, unable to perform normal math functions and arranging letters inappropriately, I was a complete disaster. I developed the strategy of moving to the back of each class, staying out of sight and, when apprehended and called upon, muttering or mumbling, "I d-d-don't kn-kn-know." That sealed my fate.

My third-grade teacher knew before I arrived that I couldn't speak, write, read or do mathematics, so she had no real optimism toward dealing with me. I discovered malingering as a basic tool to get through school. This allowed me to spend more time with the school nurse than the teacher or find vague reasons to stay home or be sent home. That was my strategy in the third and fourth grades.

Just as I was about to die intellectually, I entered the fifth grade and God placed me under the tutelage of the awesome Miss Hardy, known in the western United States as one of the most formidable elementary school teachers ever to walk the Rocky Mountains. This incredible woman, whose six-foot frame towered above me, put her arms around me and said, "He's not learning-disabled, he's eccentric."

Now, people view the potential of an

eccentric child far more optimistically than a plain old disabled one. But she didn't leave it there. She said, "I've talked with your mother and she says when she reads something to you, you remember it almost photographically. You just don't do it well when you're asked to assemble all the words and pieces. And reading out loud appears to be a problem, so when I'm going to call on you to read in my class, I'll let you know in advance so you can go home and memorize it the night before, then we'll fake it in front of the other kids. Also, Mom says when you look something over, you can talk about it with great understanding, but when she asks you to read it word for word and even write something about it, you appear to get hung up in the letters and stuff and lose the meaning. So, when the other kids are asked to read and write those worksheets I give them, you can go home, and under less pressure on your own time, do them and bring them back to me the next day."

She also said, "I notice you appear to be hesitant and fearful to express your thoughts, but I believe that any idea a person has is worth considering. I've looked into this and I'm not sure it will work, but it helped a man named Demosthenes — can you say Demosthenes?"

"D-d-d-d…"

She said, "Well, you will be able to. He had an unruly tongue, so he put stones in his mouth and practiced until he got control of it. So I've got a couple of marbles, too big to swallow, that I've washed off. From now on when I call on you, I'd like you to put them in your mouth and stand up and speak up until I can hear and understand you." And, of course, supported by her manifest belief in and understanding of me I took the risk, tamed my tongue, and was able to speak.

The next year I went on to the sixth grade, and to my delight, so did Miss Hardy. So I had the opportunity to spend two full years under her tutelage.

I kept track of Miss Hardy over the years and learned a few years ago that she was terminally ill with cancer. Knowing how lonely she would be with the only special student over 1,000 miles away, I naïvely bought a plane ticket and traveled all that distance to stand in line (at least figuratively) behind several hundred other of her special students — people who had also kept track of her and had made a pilgrimage to renew their association and share their affection for her in the latter period of her life. The group was a very interesting mix of people — three U.S. Senators, twelve state legislators and a number of chief executive officers of corporations and businesses.

The interesting thing, in comparing notes, is that three-fourths of us went into the fifth grade quite intimidated by the educational process, believing we were incapable, insignificant and at the mercy of fate or luck. We emerged from our contact with Miss Hardy believing we were capable, significant, influential people who had the capacity to make a difference in life if we would try.

Spots of a Different Color

by Grazina Smith

"*H*oney, someone left a coat in your mother's closet," I called to my husband. The faux-leopard jacket was tucked in the back of the closet against the wall, out of place among the dark coats and sweaters. I wondered who would hide clothes in my mother-in-law's closet. We were there to get a winter coat for her because she was coming home from the hospital, a week after being rushed to the emergency room.

"Coat? What coat?" My husband looked up from the mail. I took out the jacket, holding it up in the light for him to see. "Oh, that jacket. Mom bought it years ago, when I was a kid… you know, when they were fashionable. She and Pop even argued about getting it." I thought of the woman I'd know for thirty years. She bought her housedresses and polyester pantsuits at Kmart or Sears, kept her gray hair tightly confined in a hair net and chose the smallest piece of meat on the dinner platter when it was passed around the table. I knew she wasn't the kind of flamboyant type who would own a faux-leopard print jacket.

"I can't imagine Mom wearing this," I said to him.

"I don't think she ever wore it outside the house," my husband answered.

Removing the jacket from its padded hanger, I carried it to her bed and laid it on the white chenille bedspread. It seemed to sprawl like an exotic animal. My hands brushed the thick, plush fur, and the spots changed luster as my fingers sank into the pile.

My husband stood at the door. "I used to see Mom run her fingers over the fur, just like you are," he said.

As I slid my arms into the sleeves, the jacket released a perfume of gardenias and dreams. It swung loose from my shoulders, its high collar brushing my cheeks, the faux fur soft as velvet. It belonged to a glamorous, bygone era, the days of Lana Turner and Joan Crawford, but not in the closet of the practical eighty-three-year-old woman I knew.

"Why didn't you tell me Mom had a leopard jacket?" I whispered, but my husband had left the room to water the plants.

If I'd been asked to make a list of items my mother-in-law would never want in her life, that jacket would have been near the top. Yet finding it changed our relationship. It made me realize how little I knew about this woman's hopes and dreams. We took it to the hospital for her to wear home. She blushed when she saw it, and turned even rosier at the gentle teasing of the staff.

In our last three years together, I bought her gifts of perfume, lotion and makeup instead of sensible underwear and slippers. We had a lunch date once a week, where she wore her jacket, and she began to curl her hair so it would be fluffy and glamorous for our date. We spent time looking at her photo album, and I finally began to see the young woman there, with the Cupid's bow mouth.

Faux fur has come back into fashion. It appears in shop windows and on the street. Every time I catch a glimpse of it, I'm reminded of my mother-in-law's jacket, and that all of us have a secret self that needs to be encouraged and shared with those we love.

A Trucker's Last Letter

by *Rud Kendall*
Submitted by Valerie Teshima

Steamboat Mountain is a man-killer, and truckers who haul the Alaska Highway treat it with respect, particularly in the winter. The road curves and twists over the mountain and sheer cliffs drop away sharply from the icy road. Countless trucks and truckers have been lost here and many more will follow their last tracks.

On one trip up the highway, I came upon the Royal Canadian Mounted Police and several wreckers winching the remains of a semi up the steep cliff. I parked my rig and went over to the quiet group of truckers who were watching the wreckage slowly come into sight.

One of the Mounties walked over to us and spoke quietly.

"I'm sorry," he said, "the driver was dead when we found him. He must have gone over the side two days ago when we had a bad snowstorm. There weren't many tracks. It was just a fluke that we noticed the sun shining off some chrome."

He shook his head slowly and reached into his parka pocket.

"Here, maybe you guys should read this. I guess he lived for a couple of hours until the cold got to him."

I'd never seen tears in a cop's eyes before — I always figured they'd seen so much death and despair they were immune to it, but he wiped tears away as he handed me the letter. As I read it, I began to weep. Each driver silently read the words, then quietly walked back to his rig. The words were burned into my memory and now, years later, that letter is still as vivid as if I were holding it before me. I want to share that letter with you and your families.

December, 1974

My darling wife,

This is a letter that no man ever wants to write, but I'm lucky enough to have some time to say what I've forgotten to say so many times. I love you, sweetheart.

You used to kid me that I loved the truck more than you because I spent more time with her. I do love this piece of iron — she's been good to me. She's seen me through tough times and tough places. I could always count on her in a long haul and she was speedy in the stretches. She never let me down.

But you want to know something? I love you for the same reasons. You've seen me through the tough times and places, too.

Remember the first truck? That run-down 'ol' cornbinder' that kept us broke all the time but always made just enough so that we could pay the rent and the bills. Every cent I made went into the truck, while your money kept us in food with a roof over our heads.

I remember that I complained about the truck, but I don't remember you ever complaining when you came home tired from work and I asked you for money to go on the road again. If you did complain, I guess I didn't hear you. I was too wrapped up with my problems to think of yours.

I think now of all the things you gave up for me. The clothes, the holidays, the parties, the friends. You never complained and somehow I never remembered to thank you for being you.

When I sat having coffee with the boys, I always talked about my truck, my rig, my payments. I guess I forgot you were my partner even if you weren't in the cab with me. It was your sacrifices and determination as much as mine that finally got the new truck.

I was so proud of that truck I was bursting. I was proud of you too, but I never told you that. I took it for granted you knew, but if I had spent as much time talking with you as I did polishing chrome, perhaps I would have.

In all the years I've pounded the pavement, I always knew your prayers rode with me. But this time they weren't enough.

I'm hurt and it's bad. I've made my last mile and I want to say the things that should have been said so many times before. The things that were forgotten because I was too concerned about the truck and the job.

I'm thinking about the missed anniversaries and birthdays. The school plays and hockey games that you went to alone because I was on the road.

I'm thinking about the lonely nights you spent alone, wondering where I was and how things were going. I'm thinking of all the times I thought of calling you just to say hello and somehow didn't get around to. I'm thinking of the peace of mind I had knowing that you were at home with the kids, waiting for me.

The family dinners where you spent all your time telling your folks why I couldn't make it. I was busy changing oil; I was busy looking for parts; I was sleeping because I was leaving *early the next morning. There was always a reason, but somehow they don't seem very important to me right now.*

When we were married, you didn't know how to change a light bulb. Within a couple of years, you were fixing the furnace during a blizzard while I was waiting for a load in Florida. You became a pretty good mechanic, helping me with repairs, and I was mighty proud of you when you jumped into the cab and backed up over the rose bushes.

I was proud of you when I pulled into the yard and saw you sleeping in the car waiting for me. Whether it was two in the morning or two in the afternoon you always looked like a movie star to me. You're beautiful, you know. I guess I haven't told you that lately, but you are.

I made lots of mistakes in my life, but if I

only ever made one good decision, it was when I asked you to marry me. You never could understand what it was that kept me trucking. I couldn't either, but it was my way of life and you stuck with me. Good times, bad times, you were always there. I love you, sweetheart, and I love the kids.

My body hurts but my heart hurts even more. You won't be there when I end this trip. For the first time since we've been together, I'm really alone and it scares me. I need you so badly, and I know it's too late.

It's funny I guess, but what I have now is the truck. This damned truck that ruled our lives for so long. This twisted hunk of steel that I lived in and with for so many years. But it can't return my love. Only you can do that.

You're a thousand miles away but I feel you here with me. I can see your face and feel your love and I'm scared to make the final run alone.

Tell the kids that I love them very much and don't let the boys drive any truck for a living.

I guess that's about it, honey. My God, but I love you very much. Take care of yourself and always remember that I loved you more than anything in life. I just forgot to tell you.

I love you,
Bill

A Little Girl's Dream

by Jann Mitchell

*T*he promise was a long time keeping. But then, so was the dream.

In the early 1950s, in a small Southern California town, a little girl hefted yet another load of books onto the tiny library counter.

The girl was a reader. Her parents had books all over their home, but not always the ones she wanted. So she'd make her weekly trek to the yellow library with the brown trim, the little one-room building where the children's library actually was just a nook. Frequently, she ventured out of that nook in search of heftier fare.

As the white-haired librarian hand-stamped the due dates in the ten-year-old's choices, the little girl looked longingly at "The New Book" prominently displayed on the counter. She marveled again at the wonder of writing a book and having it honored like that, right there for the world to see.

That particular day, she confessed her goal.

"When I grow up," she said, "I'm going to be a writer. I'm going to write books."

The librarian looked up from her stamping and smiled, not with the condescension so many children receive, but with encouragement.

"When you do write that book," she replied, "bring it into our library and we'll put it on display, right here on the counter."

The little girl promised she would.

As she grew, so did her dream. She got her first job in ninth grade, writing brief personality profiles, which earned her $1.50 each from the local newspaper. The money paled in comparison with the magic of seeing her words on paper.

A book was a long way off.

She edited her high school paper, married and started a family, but the itch to write burned deep. She got a part-time job covering school news at a weekly newspaper. It kept her brain busy as she balanced babies.

But no book.

She went to work full-time for a major daily. Even tried her hand at magazines.

Still no book.

Finally, she believed she had something to say and started a book. She sent it off to two publishers and was rejected. She put it away, sadly. Several years later, the old dream increased in persistence. She got an agent and wrote another book. She pulled the other out of hiding, and soon both were sold.

But the world of book publishing moves slower' than that of daily newspapers, and she waited two long years. The day the box arrived on her doorstep with its author's free copies, she ripped it open. Then she cried. She'd waited so long to hold her dream in her hands.

Then she remembered that librarian's invitation, and her promise.

Of course, that particular librarian had died long ago, and the little library had been razed to make way for a larger incarnation.

The woman called and got the name of the head librarian. She wrote a letter, telling her how much her predecessor's words had meant to the girl. She'd be in town for her thirtieth high school reunion, she wrote, and could she please bring her two books by and give them to the library? It would mean so much to that ten-year-old girl, and seemed a way of honoring all the librarians who had ever encouraged a child.

The librarian called and said, "Come." So she did, clutching a copy of each book.

She found the big new library right across the street from her old high school; just opposite the room where she'd struggled through algebra, mourning the necessity of a subject that writers would surely never use, and nearly on top of the spot where her old house once stood, the neighborhood demolished for a civic center and this looming library.

Inside, the librarian welcomed her warmly. She introduced a reporter from the local newspaper—a descendant of the paper she'd begged a chance to write for long ago.

Then she presented her books to the librarian, who placed them on the counter with a sign of explanation. Tears rolled down the woman's cheeks.

Then she hugged the librarian and left, pausing for a picture outside, which proved that dreams can come true and promises can be kept. Even if it takes thirty-eight years.

The ten-year-old girl and the writer she'd become posed by the library sign, right next to the readerboard, which said:

Welcome Back, Jann Mitchell

Connection

by Susan B. Wilson

My mother and I are deeply connected by our uncanny ability to silently communicate with each other.

Fourteen years ago, I was living in Evansville, Indiana, 800 miles away from my mother…my confidante…my best friend. One morning, while in a quiet state of contemplation, I suddenly felt an urgent need to call Mother and ask if she was all right. At first I hesitated. Since my mother taught fourth grade, calling her at 5:15 A.M. could interrupt her routine and make her late for work. But something compelled me to go ahead and call her. We spoke for three minutes, and she assured me that she was safe and fine.

Later that day, the telephone rang. It was Mother, reporting that my morning phone call had probably saved her life. Had she left the house three minutes earlier, it's likely that she would have been part of a major interstate accident that killed several people and injured many more.

Eight years ago, I discovered that I was pregnant with my first child. The due date was March 15. I told the doctor that was just too soon. The baby's due date had to fall between March 29 and April 3 because that was when my mother had her spring break from teaching. And of course I wanted her with me. The doctor still insisted that the due date was mid-March. I just smiled. Reid arrived on March 30. Mother arrived on March 31.

Six years ago, I was expecting again. The doctor said the due date was toward the end of March. I said it would have to be earlier this time because — you guessed it — Mother's school break was near the beginning of March. The doctor and I both smiled. Breanne made her entry on March 8.

Two-and-a-half years ago, Mother was fighting cancer. Over time, she lost her energy, her appetite, her ability to speak. After a weekend with her in North Carolina, I had to prepare for my flight back to the Midwest. I knelt at Mother's bedside and took her hand. "Mother, if I can, do you want me to come back?" Her eyes widened as she tried to nod.

Two days later, I had a call from my stepfather. My mother was dying. Family members were gathered for last rights. They put me on a speaker phone to hear the service.

That night, I tried my best to send a loving good-bye to Mother over the miles. The next morning, however, the telephone rang:

Mother was still alive, but in a coma and expected to die any minute. But she didn't. And every day, my pain and sadness were compounded.

After four weeks passed, it finally dawned on me: Mother was waiting for me. She had communicated that she wanted me to come back if I could. I hadn't been able to before, but now I could. I made reservations immediately.

By 5:00 that afternoon, I was lying in her bed with my arms around her. She was still in a coma, but I whispered, "I'm here, Mother. You can let go. Thank you for waiting. You can let go." She died just a few hours later.

I think when a connection is that deep and powerful, it lives forever in a place far beyond words and is indescribably beautiful. For all the agony of my loss, I would not trade the beauty and power of that connection for anything.

My Mother's Hands

by Bev Hulsizer

few years ago, when my mother was visiting, she asked me to go shopping with her because she needed a new dress. I don't normally like to go shopping with other people, and I'm not a patient person, but we set off for the mall together nonetheless.

We visited nearly every store that carried ladies' dresses, and my mother tried on dress after dress, rejecting them all. As the day wore on, I grew weary and my mother grew frustrated.

Finally, at our last stop, my mother tried on a lovely blue three-piece dress. The blouse had a bow at the neckline, and as I stood in the dressing room with her, I watched as she tried, with much difficulty, to tie the bow. Her hands were so badly crippled from arthritis that she couldn't do it. Immediately, my impatience gave way to an overwhelming wave of compassion for her. I turned away to try to hide the tears that welled up involuntarily. Regaining my composure, I turned back to tie the bow for her. The dress was beautiful, and she bought it. Our shopping trip was over, but the event was etched indelibly in my memory.

For the rest of the day, my mind kept returning to that moment in the dressing room and to the vision of my mother's hands trying to tie that bow. Those loving hands that had fed me, bathed me, dressed me, caressed and comforted me, and, most of all, prayed for me, were now touching me in a most remarkable manner.

Later in the evening, I went to my mother's room, took her hands in mine, kissed them and, much to her surprise, told her that to me they were the most beautiful hands in the world.

I'm so grateful that God let me see with new eyes what a precious, priceless gift a loving, self-sacrificing mother is. I can only pray that some day my hands, and my heart, will have earned such a beauty of their own.

Remembering Ms. Murphy

by Beverly Fine

Bored with the speed and hassles of highway driving, my husband and I decided to take "the road less traveled" to the beach last summer.

A stop in a small, nondescript town on Maryland's Eastern Shore led to an incident that will forever remain in our memory.

It began simply enough. A traffic light turned red. As we waited for the signal to change, I glanced at a faded brick nursing home.

Seated on a white wicker chair on the front porch was an elderly lady. Her eyes, intent upon mine, seemed to beckon, almost implore me to come to her.

The traffic light turned green. Suddenly I blurted, "Jim, park the car around the corner."

Taking Jim's hand, I headed toward the

walkway to the nursing home. Jim stopped. "Wait a minute; we don't know anyone here." With gentle persuasion, I convinced my husband that my purpose was worthwhile.

The lady whose magnetic gaze had drawn me to her rose from her chair and, leaning on a cane, walked slowly toward us.

"I'm so glad you stopped," she smiled gratefully. "I prayed that you would. Have you a few minutes to sit and chat?" We followed her to a shady secluded spot on the side of the porch.

I was impressed by our hostess's natural beauty. She was slender, but not thin. Aside from the wrinkles at the corners of her hazel eyes, her ivory complexion was unlined, almost translucent. Her silky silver hair was tucked back neatly into a knot.

"Many people pass by here," she began, "especially in the summer. They peer from their car windows and see nothing more than an old building that houses old people. But you saw me; Margaret Murphy. And you took time to stop." Thoughtfully, Margaret said, "Some people believe that all old people are senile; the truth is that we're just plain lonely." Then, self-mockingly she said, "But we old folks do rattle on, don't we?"

Fingering a beautiful diamond-framed oval cameo on the lace collar of her floral cotton dress, Margaret asked our names and where we were from. When I said, "Baltimore," her face brightened and her eyes sparkled. She said, "My sister, bless her soul, lived on Gorusch Avenue in Baltimore all her life."

Excitedly I explained, "As a child, I lived

just a few blocks away on Homestead Street. What was your sister's name?" Immediately, I remembered Marie Gibbons. She had been my classmate and best girlfriend. For over an hour, Margaret and I shared reminiscences of our youth.

We were engaged in animated conversation when a nurse appeared with a glass of water and two small pink tablets. "I'm sorry to interrupt," she said pleasantly, "but it's time for your medication and afternoon nap, Miss Margaret. We've got to keep that ticker ticking, you know," she said, smiling and handing Margaret the medicine. Jim and I exchanged glances.

Without protest, Margaret swallowed the pills. "Can't I stay with my friends a few minutes longer, Miss Baxter?" Margaret asked. Kindly but firmly, the nurse refused.

Miss Baxter extended her arm and helped Margaret from the chair. We assured her that we would stop and see her the following week when we returned from the beach. Her unhappy expression changed to gladness. "That would be wonderful," Margaret said.

After a sunny week, the day Jim and I left for home was cloudy and damp. The nursing home seemed especially dreary under the slate-colored clouds.

After we waited a few minutes, Miss Baxter appeared. She handed us a small box with a letter attached. Then she held my hand as Jim read the letter.

Dear ones,

These past few days have been the happiest ones in my life since Henry, my beloved husband, died two years ago. Once more, I have a family I love and who cares about me.

Last night the doctor seemed concerned about my heart problem. However, I feel wonderful. And while I'm in this happy mood, I want to thank you for the joy you both have brought into my life.

Beverly dear, this gift for you is the cameo brooch I wore the day we met. My husband gave it to me on our wedding day, June 30, 1939. It had belonged to his mother. Enjoy wearing it, and I hope that someday it will belong to your daughters and their children.

With the brooch comes my everlasting love.

Margaret

Three days after our visit, Margaret died peacefully in her sleep. Teardrops stained my cheeks as I held the cameo in my hands. Tenderly, I turned it over and read the inscription engraved on the sterling silver rim of the brooch: "Love is forever."

So are memories, dear Margaret, so are memories.

On Giving Birth

by Kay Cordell Whitaker

There is something to be said about leaving a piece of yourself behind in the form of children. Twenty-seven years ago I looked upon my daughter for the first time as she was laid upon my belly, her umbilical cord still attached to me. Her little eyes seemed endless as she looked at me. I witnessed a piece of myself lying there, and yet she was so curiously and wondrously unique.

Today I stand next to her, wiping her face and reminding her to focus on the birthing movements of her own body instead of on pain and fear. She has always been utterly terrified of pain. Yet here she is…refusing all drugs…living her determination to birth her baby as nature would have it, as did the endless stream of her great-grandmothers before her.

Centuries of pushing, preparing, sighing —
and then my daughter's daughter is placed
across her mother's breast, staring into her
mother's eyes. The Great Mystery is blessing
me again, letting me see my granddaughter,
the piece of myself who will step into the
future and in turn mold her own child, my
great-grandchild.

59

She Remembered

by Lisa Boyd

*M*y mother is the sweetest, most kind-hearted person you would ever want to meet. She was always very bright and articulate, and would do anything for anyone. We've always had a close and special relationship. She is also someone whose brain is being ravaged and whose identity is being stripped away slowly because of Alzheimer's disease. She has been slipping away from us for ten years now. For me, it is a constant death, a slow letting go and a continual grieving process. Although she had lost almost all ability to care for herself, she at least still knew her immediate family. I knew the day would come when that, too, would change and finally, about two-and-a-half years ago, that day came.

My parents would visit us almost daily and

we would have a pleasant time, but suddenly there was a connection missing. My mother no longer knew me as her daughter. She would tell my father, "Oh, they are such nice people." Telling her I was her daughter made no difference at all. I had now joined the ranks of a "nice neighbor." When I would hug her good-bye, I would close my eyes and imagine that this was my mother from years ago. I would drink in every familiar sensation that I have known for thirty-six years — her warm comforting body, the squeeze of her arms and the soft, sweet smell that was hers alone.

This part of the disease was difficult for me to accept and deal with. I was going through a rough time in my life and particularly felt the need for my mother. I prayed for us both and about how much I needed her.

One late summer afternoon while I was preparing dinner, my prayers were answered and I was taken by surprise. My parents and husband were outside on the patio when my mother suddenly jumped up as if hit by a bolt of lightning. She ran into the kitchen, grabbed me gently from behind and turned me around. With a deep sense of knowledge in her eyes that seemed to transcend time and space, she tearfully and with great emotion asked me if it was true, was I her baby? Overwhelmed with emotion, I cried yes, it was true. We hugged and cried and neither of us wanted to let go of this magical moment. I knew it could disappear as quickly as it came. She said she felt a closeness to me and that I was a nice person, but that it had come to her suddenly that I was her child. We felt relief and joy. I took this gift from God and savored it, even if it were to last just for that moment or hour or day. We were given a reprieve from that awful disease and we had a special connection again. There was a sparkle back in her eyes that had been gone for a long time.

Although my mother's condition has continued to deteriorate, she remembers who I am, and it has been a year since that sweet summer afternoon. She gives me a special look and smile that seems to say, "We are in on a secret that no one else knows about." A few months ago when she was here and we had another visitor, she started stroking my hair and told them proudly, "Did you know that she was my baby?"

Baby-Lift

by LeAnn Thieman
As told to Sharon Linneá

As my friend Carol Dey and I rode through the busy streets of Saigon in a creaky VW bug on April 26, 1975, I was sure we looked exactly like what we were: a couple of Iowa homemakers. Three months earlier, when Carol and I had each agreed to escort three Vietnamese orphans to their American families, the trip seemed exciting but safe. My husband, Mark, and I had applied to adopt an orphan ourselves, in the future. We all wanted somehow to make a difference. How were Carol and I to know we would arrive just as Saigon was under siege?

Bombs were falling less than three miles from the city, and even now citizens streamed past our car, their worldly possessions tied onto pushcarts or onto their backs. But our driver, Cheri Clark, the overseas director of

Friends of the Children of Vietnam (FCVN), seemed more excited than scared. From the moment we landed, she had pelted us with unexpected news.

"Did you hear President Ford okayed a giant baby-lift as a last resort to save these children? Instead of taking out six orphans, you'll be taking home 200!" Carol and I looked at each other in amazement.

"We were able to get a planeload of children out yesterday," Cheri continued. "At the last minute, the Vietnamese government refused to let it go, but the plane was already cleared for takeoff — so it just left! That's 150 children safe in San Francisco!"

Even our years as nurses hadn't prepared us for what we found at the FCVN Center. Every inch of every floor of the stately French mansion was covered with blankets or mats—each of which was covered with babies — hundreds of crying, cooing infants, each orphaned or abandoned.

Although jet lag threatened to overwhelm us, Carol and I were determined to help prepare the children for the next day's airlift. Ours was scheduled to be the first airlift out. Each child needed clothes and diapers, a check-up and legal name. The devoted volunteers — Vietnamese and American — worked around the clock.

The next morning we learned that, in retaliation for the earlier unauthorized take-off, our agency would not be on the first flight out after all. We would be allowed to leave only when — and if — the Vietnamese government permitted.

"There's nothing we can do but wait and pray," Cheri said calmly. We all knew that time was running out for the Americans and orphans in Saigon.

In the meantime, Carol and I joined other volunteers hastily preparing children for another flight that had been cleared, this one going to Australia.

In scorching heat, we loaded babies into a VW van from which the middle seat had been removed. I sat on a bench seat with twenty-one infants packed around my feet; the others did likewise.

We arrived at the airport to find traffic at a standstill. An enormous black cloud billowed into the sky in front of us. As we passed through the gate, we heard a terrible rumor: The first planeload of orphans — the plane we had begged to be on — had crashed after takeoff.

It couldn't be true. We chose not to believe it. We had no time to worry as we went about the task of loading fussing, dehydrating babies onto the flight to freedom. Carol and I stood together holding hands while the plane took off. Once they were gone, we danced on the tarmac. One planeload was free.

Our joy was short-lived. We returned to find the adults at the center in stunned grief. Cheri haltingly confirmed what we'd refused to believe. Hundreds of babies and escorts had been killed when their plane blew apart after takeoff. No one knew if it had been shot down or bombed.

Relief workers and babies! Who could do such a thing? And would they do it again?

Overcome, I sank onto a rattan couch and sobbed uncontrollably. The plane we fought to be on had crashed, and so had my faith. I had the terrible feeling I'd never see my husband and daughters again.

That evening, Cheri beckoned me. Even in a world of drastic surprises, I was unprepared for her words: "In the satchel of papers you brought over were your adoption papers. Instead of waiting to be assigned a son, why don't you go and choose one?"

It seemed my worst fears and deepest desires came true on the same day. Wouldn't our daughters be thrilled if I came home with their new brother! But…how could I choose a child? With a prayer on my lips, I entered the next room.

As I meandered through the sea of babies,

a child crawled over to me wearing only a diaper. When I lifted him to me, he nestled his head into my shoulder and seemed to hug me back. I carried him around the room, looking at and touching each baby. Upstairs, the hall was carpeted with more infants. The little one in my arms seemed to cuddle closer as I whispered a prayer for the decision I was about to make. I felt his shallow breath as he embraced my neck and settled into my heart.

"Hello, Mitchell," I whispered to him. "I'm your mom."

The next day we got the thrilling news that our flight had been cleared to leave that afternoon. Together, all the volunteers packed up the 150 children still remaining.

Babies were placed three or four to a seat on an unused city bus for the first of several trips to the airport; Carol and I rode along. Again, a disaster. We arrived at the airport to find that Vietnamese President Thieu had canceled our flight. Trying not to panic, Carol and I helped unload the babies into filthy Quonset huts in the stifling heat. Would we never get out? Would we all die in the siege of Saigon?

Finally Ross, an FCVN worker, burst in. "President Thieu is allowing only one flight, and it's got to leave immediately. Let's get these babies loaded on — and you, too!" he said to Carol and me. Our chance to leave!

"No," I said. "I left my son back at the center for a later bus. I've got to go back and get him."

"LeAnn," Ross said, "you see how things are. Leave while you can. I promise we'll try to get your son out to you."

Yes, I saw how things were. "I won't leave without Mitchell!"

"Hurry, then," Ross said. "I'll hold the plane as long as I can, but we can't ruin these other children's chances."

I ran to the bus. The driver screeched recklessly through the chaotic city and delivered me a mile from the center. The strap of my sandal broke and the shoe flapped wildly against my ankle. I took it off while still running. My side ached fiercely as I raced up the stairs to the center.

"The plane..." I gasped as Cheri eased me into a chair. "I know. I just got off the phone with the airport."

"And?"

Cheri grinned. "The plane will wait for you!"

I beamed a smile while gasping for breath.

"Not only that — we can take more babies for this flight — and a second flight has been approved, as well!"

Tears streaming down my face, I found Mitchell and held him close. I made a silent vow never to leave him again.

A few hours later, I felt my heart pound as I boarded a gutted cargo plane. Twenty cardboard boxes formed a row down the center, with two to three infants per box. Toddlers and older children sat belted on the long side benches, bewilderment on their faces.

The doors were closed; the engine's roar was deafening. I couldn't remove the image of the black cloud from the downed plane from my mind. A panic came over me and I gripped Mitchell closer. I prayed the Lord's Prayer as the plane taxied down the runway. Then...

we were airborne. If we could only live through the next five minutes, I knew we'd make it home.

Finally the captain spoke. "We're out of artillery range. We're safe. We're going home!" Shouts of joy filled the plane.

As I thought of the chaos of war, I prayed for those we'd left behind. And then I uttered a prayer of thanks that Carol and I had been allowed to make a difference, in a bigger way than we'd ever dreamed. We were all headed for lives filled with new hope — including the son I hadn't known I had.